kids cooking

KIDS

by Aileen Paul

COOKING

the
Aileen Paul
Cooking School
Cookbook

and Arthur Hawkins

Doubleday & Company, Inc.   Garden City   New York

Library of Congress Catalog Card Number 78–89105
Copyright © 1970 by Doubleday & Company, Inc.
All Rights Reserved
Printed in the United States of America
First Edition

S   1535020

to—
Celia
Jesse
Katie
Ralph
Linda
Fred
Belinda
Matthew
Artie
Mary
Frankie
Betty
Herbie
Nancy
Bill
Barbara
Gil
Liza
Joe
Suzie
Dick
Kathie
Julian
.

.

.

.

contents

introduction
for mothers

Cooking is an exciting and novel
experience for children. Whether
they're making chili con carne or hot
buttered popcorn, the act of cooking
provides an instant entry into the
adult world.

Since nothing succeeds like success,
children should begin cooking with
simple short recipes. If they attempt
too much to begin with, like adults
they become flustered. In my cooking
classes, which meet once a week for
an hour, we prepare just one dish.
And you will find that most of the
recipes in this book can be completed,
and the kitchen tidied again in about
one hour.

It is of course very important for children to learn the technique of cooking—the order in which ingredients are added, kneading, mixing, etc. But far from these techniques being a bore, I find that children really enjoy learning them—particularly when there is a clearly explained reason and purpose behind them.

For example, one week my cooking class may learn to scramble eggs. They carefully break the eggs into a bowl and beat them lightly with a wire whisk. At the same time we will discuss the other methods of beating eggs and the occasions upon which they should be used. In the next class the children build on their knowledge when they prepare meringue cookies using egg whites only. They separate the yolks and the whites this time, beat the egg yolks stiffly with an electric mixer. All the time they're developing new skills and learning new techniques—and thoroughly enjoying themselves in the process.

Children are eager to try the tools of cooking, from simple measuring spoons to complicated utensils. Hand a ten-year-old a professional pastry bag with tips and tubes to design rosettes and leaves, and watch his interest rise. The routines of cooking, which adults take for granted, are exciting adventures for children. Although you and I may pay little attention to a tossed salad we make, for a twelve-year-old this can be a truly enjoyable task.

A brief word about equipment. I am assuming that you have the usual spatulas, pots and pans, etc., but I think I should mention that the children in my class find cooking easier when they have glass measuring cups of various sizes: 1-cup, 2-cup, and 4-cup. Such equipment is inexpensive and makes for easier preparations. Although most households probably do not have a candy or deep-fat thermometer, they are helpful and I would recommend their purchase.

a note to kids

12   Cooking is fun; it's a game. But like all games there are certain rules to be followed. Since the rules of the kitchen are so important, you and your mother should read these notes together.

RULES OF THE GAME

1. Turn handles of pots and pans you are using so that neither you nor anyone else will knock them off the stove or counter.

2. Use a dry pot holder when you place things in the oven and when you take them out. A damp pot holder is no protection against heat.

3. Use a paring knife (that's the little one that sometimes has a saw-toothed edge) for most of your cutting; for sandwiches use a bread knife.

4. Use a wooden chopping board for cutting. Most counter tops scratch easily.

Adults can be useful to you in the kitchen so, depending on your age, let your "assistant" do the following:

1. Turn on the oven or the burners of the stove.

2. Stand by in case you need help when you are using the oven.

3. Pour hot water for you when needed.

13

There's one rule that the kids in my cooking classes have never broken, and I'm sure you won't either: Use the electric mixer or blender *only* when an adult is right there by you.

There are certain steps which must be taken:

Step **1.** Read the recipe carefully. The recipes are chosen for ages seven to twelve, but what you can cook depends upon how much cooking you have done, and not on your age.

Step **2.** Check the list of ingredients to be sure you have everything you need *before* you start.

Step 3. Place together the ingredients and the equipment you will need such as:

> measuring cups
> measuring spoons
> wooden spoons and rubber spatulas
> mixing bowls

Step 4. Place a damp sponge in a convenient spot to wipe up the spills that are bound to come. (Don't worry about them.)

breakfast dishes

CEREAL SURPRISE

CINNAMON TOAST

BAKED EGGS

EGGS IN A NEST

SCRAMBLED EGGS

FRENCH TOAST

FRIED HAM SLICE

15

cereal surprise

There's a special flavor in cooked cereal that is missing in prepared dry cereals. Oatmeal, for example, is delicious cooked according to directions on the package, or you can easily add an extra-delicious taste with Cereal Surprise.

here's what you need

½ teaspoon salt

⅔ cup quick-cooking oat-meal

favorite jam or jelly

medium-sized saucepan
with matching cover (2-quart)

1-cup glass measuring cup

2-cup glass measuring cup

measuring spoons

long-handled mixing
spoon, wooden or metal

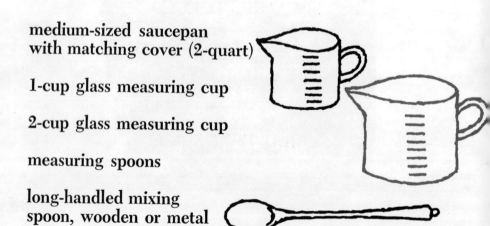

here's what you do

1. Find 1½-cup mark on 2-cup measuring cup. Run water from faucet slowly into cup until measuring line is reached.

2. Pour measured water into saucepan. Measure ½ teaspoon salt and add to water.

3. Place saucepan over high heat. Let water boil (begin to bubble up).

4. Measure ⅔ cup of oatmeal in 1-cup measuring cup. Stir oatmeal into boiling water, using long-handled spoon. Cook for 1 minute over medium heat, stirring now and then.

17

5. Remove pan from heat and cover immediately. Let oatmeal "rest" for 2 minutes away from the heat. Actually, cereal holds heat and continues to cook during this time.

6. Rinse 1-cup measuring cup that you used. Spoon favorite jam or jelly into cup until ¼-cup measuring line is reached.

7. Remove cover from saucepan. Swirl jam or jelly through cereal with mixing spoon.

8. Serve immediately while steaming hot.

Makes 2 servings

cinnamon toast

Here are two ways of preparing Cinnamon Toast. One is for those allowed to use the oven and the other is for those whose mothers prefer that they use the toaster. You need the same ingredients for each, and the result tastes almost the same.

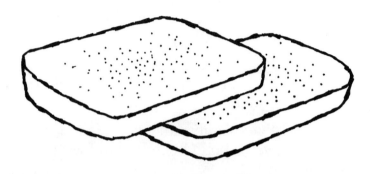

18 here's what you need

1 teaspoon cinnamon

3 tablespoons sugar

4 slices white bread

¼ cup (½ stick) softened butter

measuring spoons

small bowl

table knife or small spatula

cookie sheet

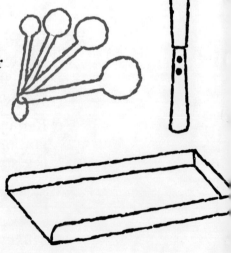

here's what you do

Toaster Method

1. Measure cinnamon and sugar into bowl. Stir with wooden mixing spoon until blended.*

2. Toast bread in toaster. Butter right away and sprinkle with cinnamon-sugar mixture.

Oven Method

1. Preheat oven to 375°.

2. Measure cinnamon and sugar into mixing bowl. Stir with wooden mixing spoon until blended. Add softened butter and blend again.

3. Place slices of bread on cookie sheet.

4. Spread cinnamon mixture on slices. Place cookie sheet in oven and bake until lightly brown, about 5 minutes. Use hot pads when you remove cookie sheet from oven.

Makes 2 servings

* To blend means to mix two or more ingredients until they appear to be one.

baked eggs

If you want to fix breakfast for several people, baked eggs (also called shirred eggs) are convenient because the eggs stay hot longer in a baking dish than on a plate.

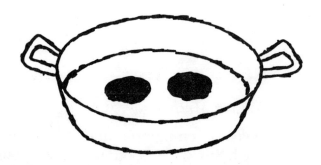

here's what you need

2 tablespoons butter

4 eggs

4 tablespoons light or heavy cream

salt and pepper

small custard dishes or large shallow baking dish

measuring spoons

table knife or small spatula

aluminum foil

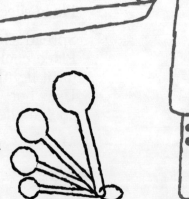

here's what you do

1. Preheat oven to 325°.

2. Grease baking dish or custard dishes.

3. Break 1 egg into each dish; or all 4 eggs into shallow baking dish. Take care to keep yolk unbroken.

4. Measure and add 1 tablespoon cream for each egg. Sprinkle with salt and pepper. Using knife, place 3 small bits of butter, about the size of a dime, on each egg. Cover each dish with a piece of aluminum foil.

5. Place in oven and bake 12 to 18 minutes, depending upon how hard cooked you like your eggs.
     (If you are using individual baking dishes, it will be easier to place them in oven if dishes are together on a cookie sheet.)

6. Remove from oven, using hot pads, and place baking dish or dishes on plates to serve.

Makes 4 servings

eggs in a nest

There are several ways to prepare Eggs in a Nest. This is the one my cooking class likes best.

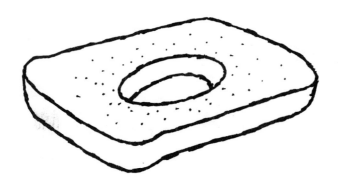

here's what you need

1 slice white bread per person

butter

1 egg per person

salt and pepper

large frying pan with cover

wooden chopping board

2-inch-round cookie cutter

cup or small bowl

broad metal spatula

here's what you do

1. Place bread slices on chopping board.

2. Cut circles in each slice of bread with 2-inch cookie cutter. (Store circles of bread in plastic bag to use another time for sandwiches.)

3. Place frying pan over medium heat.

4. Melt butter in frying pan, enough to cover bottom, about 2 tablespoons.

5. Fry bread slices on one side in melted butter. Turn slices over with spatula. Add more butter if pan becomes dry.

6. Lower heat.

7. Break eggs, one at a time, into cup and pour each egg gently into bread ring. Season with salt and pepper.

8. Place cover on frying pan and cook until eggs are as firm as you want, about 3 to 5 minutes.

Makes 1 for each person

scrambled eggs

When you are cooking eggs, always use low or medium heat. Remember that eggs should be served as quickly as possible after they are cooked.

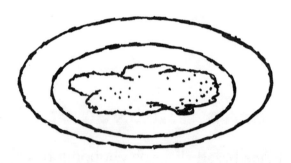

here's what you need

eggs, usually 3 for 2 people

milk or water

salt and pepper

butter

frying pan

bowl

whisk, rotary beater, or fork

rubber spatula

here's what you do

1. Break eggs into bowl.

2. To each 3 eggs, add 3 tablespoons milk or water, ½ teaspoon salt, dash of pepper.

3. Beat eggs with whisk, rotary beater, or fork until yolks and whites are thoroughly mixed but not frothy.

4. Place frying pan on moderate heat, and add about 2 tablespoons of butter, enough to cover bottom of pan.

5. Add beaten eggs. Use a rubber spatula to scrape eggs from sides and bottom of skillet gently but quickly as they cook.

6. Cook eggs the way you like them, creamy and soft, or dry and fluffy. It's up to you.

7. Serve immediately.

Scramble 3 eggs for every 2 people

french toast

Everyone likes French toast. It tastes good, it's good for you, and it's easy to make.

here's what you need

1 egg

⅓ cup milk

1 tablespoon sugar

pinch of salt

½ teaspoon vanilla

6 slices white bread, cut in half

about ¼ cup butter (½ stick)

large frying pan

1 medium mixing bowl

egg beater or whisk

measuring spoons

long-handled fork or tongs

broad metal spatula

here's what you do

1. Break egg into bowl.

2. Measure milk, sugar, salt, and vanilla into bowl.

3. Beat with egg beater, or whisk, until yolk and white are blended, but not too frothy.

4. Place frying pan on medium heat. Add butter to cover bottom of pan when melted, usually 2 tablespoons are enough.

5. Dip pieces of bread, using tongs or fork, into egg mixture. Place in skillet.

6. Fry bread until golden brown on one side. Turn with spatula and fry on other side. Add more butter as needed.

7. Serve with jam, jelly, or syrup.

Makes 4 servings

fried ham slice

If you like a big breakfast, how about including ham? A ham slice is easy to cook because it needs to be turned only once.

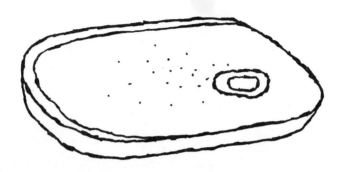

here's what you need

1 center-cut ham slice,
¼ to ½ inch thick

> (*Ham slices are often prepackaged at the meat counter*)

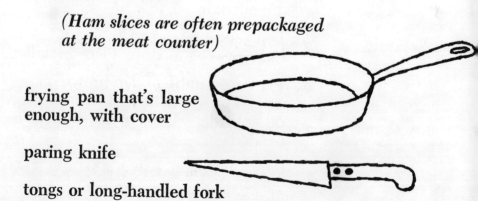

frying pan that's large enough, with cover

paring knife

tongs or long-handled fork

here's what you do

1. Place frying pan over medium heat.

2. Trim fat from ham slice, leaving about ⅛ inch of fat on edge. Cut into edge of fat, every inch around, to keep ham from curling. Place trimmed fat in frying pan. Stir with kitchen fork for 2 or 3 minutes while fat melts.

3. Remove pieces of unmelted fat from frying pan and put in ham slice.

4. Fry on one side 3 to 5 minutes for uncooked ham. Turn and fry same time on other side. (If ham is precooked, fry 2 minutes on each side.)

   If you also want eggs, fry ham first. Remove frying pan from heat and cover immediately. Ham will stay warm while you fry or scramble eggs in a separate frying pan.

   1 pound of ham serves 2 people generously

things to remember

When you have finished using dishes or pans, place in sink and fill with warm sudsy water. Washing will be easier later because food doesn't stick.

Keep eggs in refrigerator, and take out only the amount needed.

The groceries listed may say "butter or margarine" and the instructions say "butter." That's because I feel you might get tired of repeatedly hearing "butter or margarine." You may cook with either one. Butter is an animal fat, more expensive; margarine is a vegetable fat, less expensive than butter. Both have vitamins A and D.

Keep dry hot pads handy.

Rinse egg beater or whisk with warm water, never hot, immediately after using.

lunch dishes

GRILLED CHEESE SANDWICHES

GRILLED PEANUT
BUTTER SANDWICHES

BEEF AND MACARONI

31

RIBBON SANDWICHES

ALL KINDS OF SOUP

HOMEMADE VEGETABLE SOUP

TUNA FISH BOATS

grilled cheese sandwiches

*Would you like grilled cheese sandwiches for lunch?
You can use any type of cheese you prefer: American,
Swiss, Cheddar. Take a look at the varieties when you go
to the grocery store.*

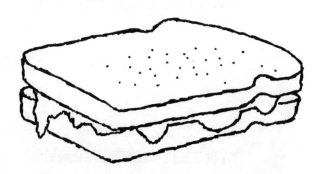

32

here's what you need

8 slices bread for 4
sandwiches

prepared mustard

butter

4 slices cheese

table knife

frying pan

here's what you do

1. On 4 slices of bread, spread mustard.

2. On remaining 4 slices, spread softened butter.

3. Place 4 slices of cheese on 4 slices of bread and top with remaining bread.

4. Place frying pan on medium heat. Add small amount of butter to cover bottom of pan, enough so that sandwiches will not stick.

5. Place sandwiches in heated frying pan. The average-sized pan will hold 2 or 3.

6. Fry on one side until golden. Turn with spatula and fry on other side.

grilled peanut butter sandwiches

Try peanut butter sandwiches grilled for a different taste.

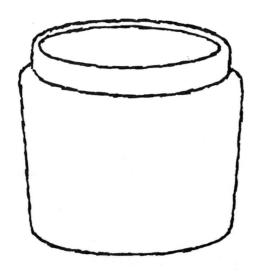

here's what you need

8 slices bread for 4
sandwiches

butter

peanut butter

jelly or ham slice, if you want

table knife

frying pan

pancake turner

S 1535020

here's what you do

1. On 4 slices of bread, spread peanut butter. If you want, you may add your favorite jam or jelly. You may also skip the jelly and add a thin slice of boiled ham instead.

2. On remaining 4 slices of bread, spread softened butter.

3. Place frying pan on medium heat. Add small amount of butter to cover bottom of pan, enough so that sandwiches will not stick.

4. Place sandwiches in heated frying pan. Average frying pan will hold 2 or 3.

5. Fry on one side until golden. Turn with spatula and fry on other side.

beef and macaroni

Sometimes you and your friends are especially hungry at lunch time. Here's an easy recipe that really fills you up.

36

here's what you need

1 pound ground boneless chuck or 1 pound hamburger

1 tablespoon butter

1 teaspoon onion salt

1 can prepared macaroni with cheese sauce

frying pan

wooden spoon or long-handled kitchen fork

measuring spoon

here's what you do

1. Place frying pan over low heat. Add 1 tablespoon butter, or enough to cover bottom of pan.

2. After butter has melted, put ground beef into skillet. Stir with wooden spoon, or long-handled fork, keeping meat in small pieces, not chunks. Cook until meat loses red color, but not until brown.

3. Open can of macaroni and add to meat. Sprinkle with onion salt, stir, and heat until steaming.

Serves 4 to 6

ribbon sandwiches

Ribbon sandwiches are pretty. They are nice to serve for guests at lunch, and especially nice for birthdays. You can make ribbon sandwiches a day ahead and keep them in the refrigerator in airtight wrapping.

here's what you need

2 cans deviled ham
(4½ ounces each)

2 packages whipped cream cheese (4 ounces each)

9 slices thin-sliced whole-wheat bread

6 slices thin-sliced white bread

> *(Buy same "kind" of bread so that slices will match; some loaves are more curved than others)*

small mixing bowl

wooden mixing spoon

table knife or spatula for spreading

bread knife

transparent plastic wrap

here's what you do

1. Mix deviled ham and cream cheese in a bowl with wooden mixing spoon.

2. Place opened packages of bread by bread board. Remove 3 slices of whole-wheat and 2 slices of white, leaving the rest of bread in package to stay fresh.

3. Spread filling on 2 slices of whole-wheat and 2 slices of white bread.

4. Begin stack with first slice of whole-wheat, add white slice, then whole-wheat, then white. Top with whole-wheat slice on which there is no filling.

5. Wrap in transparent plastic wrap and chill about 30 minutes. Sandwiches may be placed in freezer for 10 minutes to speed chilling.
    (The reason for chilling fancy sandwiches is to make them easier to cut.)

6. Repeat process until you have three stacks.

7. After sandwiches are thoroughly chilled, remove wrapping, cut off crusts using bread knife, and slice through stack in 1-inch strips. Cut each strip again in half. Serve immediately or return to the refrigerator until needed.

Makes approximately 24 sandwiches, enough for 7 or 8 people.

all kinds of soups

Let me give you a few suggestions about preparing canned and packaged soups since soup and sandwiches are young America's favorite lunch.

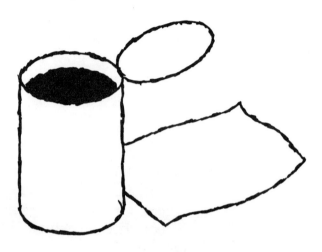

here's what you need

can of condensed soup
                or
package of soup mix

saucepan, 2-quart size
wire whisk if you have one
        *(Whisks are inexpensive and can be bought
        at most hardware or department stores)*

narrow rubber spatula

ladle or large spoon for serving

here's what you do

1. You add different amounts of water to canned soup and to package soup mix. Read and follow instructions on label or package. They are usually quite clear.

2. Bring soup up to boiling point. Do not boil. Lower heat immediately so that soup simmers. The taste changes with rapid boiling.

3. You can, if you want, add extra ingredients to prepared soups. Here are a few suggestions:

   To bean soup, add 2 tablespoons or ½ cup tomato sauce.

   To tomato soup, add ½ cup cooked rice or ¼ cup raisins.

   To chicken or vegetable soup, add one of the following garnishes which may be chopped on wooden board or cut very fine with scissors: 1 tablespoon chopped mint or parsley.

1 can soup or 1 package makes 4 servings

homemade vegetable soup

Make this soup on a rainy day when you want to stay inside and maybe have a friend over. In between cooking steps, you can play games, work with clay, or prepare a simple dessert.

here's what you need

2 stalks celery   3 carrots

2 beef bones from cooked rib roast

2 pieces bay leaf

1 tablespoon onion powder
or onion salt

1 large can tomatoes

1 can okra (1 pound) or
1 package frozen okra (10 ounces)

⅛ cup barley   ½ cup rice

Tabasco sauce   salt and pepper

1 large soup kettle

1 wooden mixing spoon

paring knife

measuring spoons

chopping board

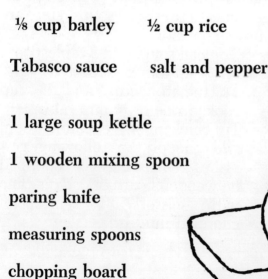

here's what you do

1. Scrub carrots and celery under running water with brush.

2. Place 2 whole carrots, 1 stalk celery, beef bones, bay leaf, and onion powder or salt in soup kettle. Add water to cover.

3. Place on high heat until water comes to boil. Lower heat, cover, and simmer for 2 hours.

4. Stir about every 20 minutes. Add water if needed to cover vegetables.

5. After simmering, liquid is transformed into beef stock, the base for soup. Discard whole vegetables, whose purpose was to add flavor.

6. Bring stock to boil with addition of following vegetables: tomatoes, okra, barley, and rice. Then lower and simmer for ¾ hour.

7. Slice and add remaining carrot and celery.

8. Soup is ready when carrots and celery are tender but crisp, about 15 minutes.

9. Add salt and pepper to taste, and dash of Tabasco sauce.

Makes 8 to 10 servings

tuna fish boats

*Sandwich boats are fun to make for friends or family.
You can use any filling you like, but most kids like tuna.*

here's what you need

1 can tuna fish (6½ or 7 ounces)

several stalks celery

¼ cup mayonnaise or
bottled lemon juice and
softened butter

uncut long rolls, soft
like frankfurter rolls or
hero bread rolls

parsley if you want it

strainer

mixing bowl

wooden chopping board

rubber spatula or mixing spoon

regular paring knife

grapefruit knife

tablespoon

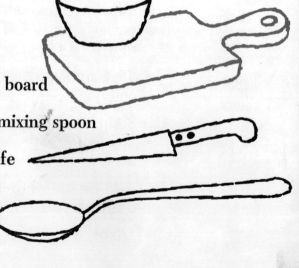

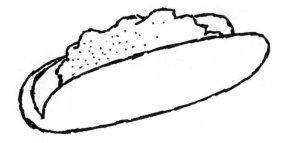

here's what you do

1. Open can of tuna fish and drain liquid through strainer directly into sink.

2. To chop celery, hold stalk at leafy end on chopping board. Slice lengthwise with regular paring knife to about 1 inch from end. Slice crosswise. Measure ½ cup.

3. In bowl, combine tuna, celery, and mayonnaise.
   (If you don't like mayonnaise, sprinkle tuna mixture with 2 teaspoons bottled lemon juice and blend in 2 or 3 tablespoons softened butter.)

4. Prepare "boats" by hollowing inside of roll (leaving ½ inch shell) with type of paring knife that is sometimes called a grapefruit knife. It has a curved blade.

5. Fill boats with tuna mixture. Decorate with sprig of parsley.

Makes 4 or 5 sandwiches, depending upon size of rolls

things to remember

To grill means to cook by direct heat, usually on griddle or grill, with only enough fat added to keep foods from sticking. I find the frying pan better for children than a griddle or grill because it offers more protection.

If you want to know how many sandwiches to prepare, plan on 1½ sandwiches per person. In other words, 3 sandwiches for 2 people.

There are many delicious breads at the grocery store and bakery. Try a new type such as cracked wheat, whole-wheat, or different styles of rye breads. The flavors are delicious and these breads contain the important food elements that help you play a better game of ball, swim longer, and have a better complexion.

You can prepare uncooked sandwiches in advance. Keep them fresh by wrapping in moisture-proof paper and storing in refrigerator.

dinner dishes

CHILI CON CARNE

HAMBURGERS

MEAT LOAF

BAKED POTATO

ROAST BEEF DINNER

TOSSED GREEN SALAD

SPAGHETTI AND MEAT

chili con carne

You probably know that chili con carne, a very spicy Mexican dish, means chili beans with meat. It is very popular in many parts of our country.

here's what you need

2 medium-sized onions   1 garlic clove

3 tablespoons vegetable oil

1 pound ground boneless chuck beef

1 can tomato sauce (8 ounces)

1 can red kidney beans (1 pound)

Spices ½ teaspoon celery salt   1 bay leaf

48

¼ teaspoon red pepper   ⅛ teaspoon basil

½ teaspoon caraway seed   1½ teaspoons salt

1 tablespoon chili powder

1 large deep frying pan

wooden spoon

chopping board

chopping knife or paring knife

measuring spoons

small paper cup

here's what you do

1. To chop onion: peel off outer layer. (Some people place onion under running water while peeling to help avoid tears!) Place onion on side on chopping board. With knife, which can be a paring knife if it is easier for you to handle, cut thin slice off root end. Grip onion around stem end and cut lengthwise as far as you can go comfortably. Cut onion crosswise again as far as you can.

2. Peel garlic clove and leave whole.

3. Place frying pan over low heat. Pour in enough oil to cover bottom. Heat oil for several minutes. Add ground beef, chopped onions and whole garlic clove. Cook until beef has lost its red color, about 3 to 5 minutes.

4. While beef is cooking, measure spices and salt into a small cup for convenience.

5. After beef is cooked, about 5 minutes, add can of tomato sauce and mixed spices and salt. Simmer 1 hour. Stir occasionally.

6. Remove garlic clove.

7. Add red kidney beans and heat 10 minutes.

Makes 4 to 6 servings

hamburgers

At the meat counter buy 1 pound of hamburger or ground boneless chuck beef. If meat is prepackaged, you will find weight on package and also type of beef.

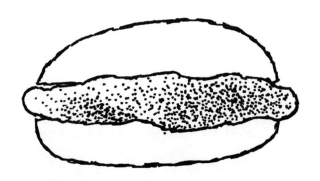

here's what you need

1 pound ground hamburger
or ground boneless chuck

small amount of shortening

salt and pepper

4 hamburger rolls

large frying pan

broad metal spatula

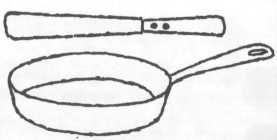

here's what you do

1. Divide ground beef into 4 equal sections, using knife.

2. Shape into balls, gently using finger tips. The less you handle meat the better.

3. Flatten out balls again, using finger tips, not palms of hand. You should have 4 patties, each ½ inch thick.

4. Rub frying pan lightly with shortening.

5. Heat pan over medium to high heat.

6. Place meat patties in pan and brown on one side. Turn with spatula and brown on other side.

7. Immediately lower heat and continue cooking until done, about 5 minutes more for those who like hamburger rare, 10 minutes more for those who like medium, and 12 minutes more for well done.

8. Season after cooking with salt and pepper. Serve on rolls.

Makes 4 servings

meat loaf

Here is a basic meat loaf recipe which my classes use. Basic means it has all of the important ingredients. However, you can exchange certain ingredients. For example, you may exchange liquids, such as tomato juice or beef bouillon, for tomato sauce. I have not included chopped onions because many children do not like them in meat loaf.

here's what you need

½ cup tomato sauce   1 egg

1½ cups bread crumbs

2 pounds ground beef or
prepackaged meat loaf mixture

2 teaspoons salt

sprinkle of pepper

loaf pan or casserole dish

large mixing bowl

egg beater

table fork

1-cup measuring cup

2-cup measuring cup

measuring spoons

here's what you do

1. Lightly grease loaf pan or casserole dish.

2. Preheat oven to 350°.

3. Break egg into large bowl and add tomato sauce. Beat with egg beater until fluffy.

53

4. Prepare bread crumbs from 4 to 6 slices of white bread.

5. Add beef, salt, and pepper. Stir gently with fork until ingredients are blended.

6. Pat mixture into oval shape, like a football.

7. Place meat loaf in pan, keeping oval shape. Bake 1 hour and 15 minutes. If there is time, let stand 15 minutes before serving; this makes slicing easier.

Makes 6 to 8 servings

baked potatoes

If you want to prepare a complete meal, you could have meat loaf, tossed green salad, and baked potato. You buy a special variety for baking, usually either an Idaho baking potato or a Maine baking potato.

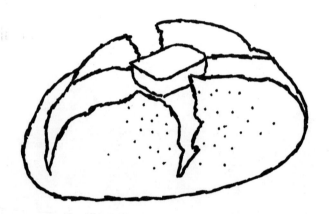

here's what you need

4 baking potatoes

butter

salt

hot pads

here's what you do

1. Preheat oven to 425°.

2. Wash potatoes under running water, scrubbing with vegetable brush. The skins must be clean, as they are very good to eat. Dry with towel.

3. Rub butter or vegetable shortening over each potato, using finger tips or folded piece of wax paper or paper towel.

55

4. Place potatoes on oven rack, not too close together.

5. Bake until done (about 45 minutes). Remove 1 potato from oven, using hot pads, and squeeze potato gently with towel. If soft, potatoes are done. If still hard, return to oven for another 5 or 10 minutes to finish baking.

6. When potatoes are done, remove from oven, using hot pads.

7. Cut slits crosswise on top of each potato to allow steam to escape, and place a piece of butter on opened potato.

Allow 1 potato per person

roast beef dinner

Roast beef is delicious and easy to fix for a weekend dinner. You can go to the butcher and ask for a 2-rib standing rib roast. Be sure to have him mark the weight on the package so that you can cook beef the right length of time.

here's what you need

2-rib standing rib roast of beef

1 can potatoes (1 pound)

1 can carrots or green
beans (1 pound)

1 can onions (1 pound)

large roasting pan

large serving platter

2 cooking forks

cooking spoon

here's what you do

1. Preheat oven to 300°.

2. Place beef, fat side up, in open roasting pan. You may need to place it on rack to keep beef standing. Do not add water. Let people add salt and pepper when they are eating.

3. Figure cooking time from this chart:

rare	20 minutes per pound
medium rare	25 minutes per pound
well done	30 minutes per pound

If your roast is 8 pounds, and you want it medium rare, multiply 8 by 25, which gives you 200 minutes. Divide by 60 (60 minutes to the hour, right?) and you learn that the roast should cook 3 hours and 20 minutes.

4. Half an hour before roast is finished, open cans of vegetables, drain liquid, pour vegetables slowly into roasting pan so that juice does not splatter.

5. At serving time, you'll need someone to help you take pan from oven because it will be hot and heavy.

6. Remove roast first, using two forks, and place on serving dish. Then add vegetables.

1 pound of meat serves 2 or 3

tossed green salad

There are different kinds of salad. This one is a green salad, which goes with a main dish, either at lunch or dinner.

here's what you need

salad greens of your choice: iceberg, Bibb, or Boston lettuce (I have left out salad greens that need a lot of washing)

salt and pepper

58 olive oil or vegetable oil of the best quality

vinegar (preferably wine vinegar) or lemon juice

you may want to add

celery

radishes or cucumbers

tomatoes

salad bowl

salad fork and spoon

here's what you do

1. Wash head of lettuce under faucet, using coldest water. Pat dry gently with paper towel. Discard outer lettuce leaves if discolored or bruised. Wrap head of lettuce in paper towel or cloth towel to absorb moisture. Chill in refrigerator if there is time.

2. Place lettuce, torn into bite-sized pieces, in salad bowl.

3. Add any of the vegetables you want (see instructions below).

4. Sprinkle salad with salt and pepper.

5. Prepare dressing by pouring 2 tablespoons oil into large salad spoon. (You can rest it lightly on greens.) Sprinkle oil over greens and toss. Pour 1 tablespoon vinegar into wooden spoon, sprinkle over greens, and toss.
   (You can mix oil and vinegar in wooden spoon and then sprinkle, but that takes a bit of practice).

6. You can prepare salad 3 to 4 hours in advance without dressing. Cover with transparent plastic wrap—make it airtight—and refrigerate until ready to serve.

Vegetables

Scrub with vegetable brush under running cold water.
> Place on chopping board:
> celery—slice diagonally,
> radishes or cucumbers—slice,
> tomatoes—cut in wedges.

59

spaghetti and meat

When you plan to cook the entire meal, you must decide how you will spend your time. You would have more time to spend on dessert, for example, if you spent less time on the main dish. This casserole of spaghetti and meat is easy and quick.

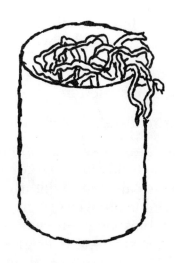

here's what you need

1 can prepared spaghetti
with sauce (15 ounces)

1 can Vienna sausage (4
ounces), or 1 can luncheon
meat (12 ounces)

½ cup prepared bread crumbs

casserole

cooking fork

here's what you do

1. Preheat oven to 350°.

2. Lightly grease casserole.

3. Pour ½ can prepared spaghetti into casserole.

4. Sprinkle with half of crumbs.

5. Place Vienna sausage, or sliced canned luncheon meat, over spaghetti, several inches apart.

6. Add final layer of spaghetti and crumbs.

7. Bake 20 to 30 minutes.

Makes 4 servings

things to remember

Keep your menu simple if you plan the entire dinner—a meat, potatoes (or a hearty combination like chili), vegetable, a salad, and fruit for dessert.

Let's talk about buying ground beef, which is used in many of the recipes. You may buy regular ground beef called hamburger (less expensive with a little more fat); ground boneless chuck, which costs a little more; or ground round steak, which has very little, if any, fat and is the most expensive. The best buy is usually ground boneless chuck. If meat is prepackaged in your store, the label will identify it.

An easy way to grease a casserole or baking pan is to place a piece of paper towel or wax paper around your hand. Dip into shortening or softened butter. Rub utensil thoroughly, sides and bottom.

Always, always use pot holders when you handle hot pans. The smaller size is probably better for you. Try the pot holder in your own hand to check fit.

dessert dishes

ICE CREAM WITH
CHOCOLATE SAUCE

GLAZED ICE CREAM BALLS

JELL-O GELATIN DESSERTS

FUNNY-FACE CUPCAKES

PEANUT BUTTER BAR COOKIES

RAISIN PUDDING

WACKY CAKE

ice cream with chocolate sauce

Ice cream with chocolate sauce is everybody's favorite. Chocolate sauce is easy to prepare, and there's very little cleaning to do afterwards, which is rather nice for a change.

here's what you need

1 package German sweet chocolate* (4 ounces)

5 tablespoons water

¼ cup sugar

dash salt

1 tablespoon butter

¼ teaspoon vanilla

ice cream of your choice

double boiler

measuring spoons

rubber spatula

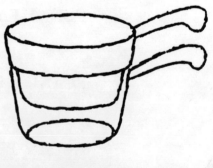

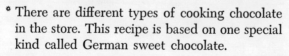

* There are different types of cooking chocolate in the store. This recipe is based on one special kind called German sweet chocolate.

here's what you do

1. Run water into the lower part of the double boiler. There should be enough water so that the top part of the double boiler rests about ½ inch above the water.

2. Place on high heat until water boils, then lower heat to medium.

3. Break bar of chocolate in squares directly into top of double boiler.

4. Add water, sugar, and salt to chocolate.

5. Cook and stir until sauce is smooth.

6. Remove from heat. Stir in butter and vanilla. Let cool slightly.

7. Scoop ice cream in sherbert glass and pour sauce over it.

Makes 1½ cups sauce

glazed ice cream balls

This is a simple dessert all dressed up. Once you have tried my recipe, you can make changes in the ingredients. For example I use frozen orange juice, but, at another time, try other frozen juices. Or you could substitute flaked coconut for walnuts.

here's what you need

1 cup shelled walnuts

2 cans frozen concentrated orange juice (6 ounces each)

quart vanilla ice cream

cookie sheet

ice-cream scoop

slotted spoon or 2 forks

metal spatula

medium-sized bowl

paper plate or piece of wax paper. Paper plates are handy when preparing food. The rim around the edges keeps things from sliding around too much.

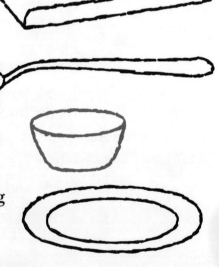

transparent freezer wrap

here's what you do

1. Chop nuts very fine on wooden board with a knife, or use a nut chopper, or grind in blender. Pour on paper plate.

2. Prepare glaze by blending 2 containers frozen orange juice with 2 containers water in large mixing bowl.

3. Line up in following order:
   1—ice cream
   2—glaze in bowl
   3—chopped nuts on paper plate
   4—cookie sheet covered with transparent freezer wrap

4. Ready? Scoop ice cream, one rounded ball at a time, and drop into glaze. Gently stir until covered with glaze. Use a slotted spoon or two forks to remove balls from glaze. Drain extra glaze over bowl.

5. Roll in ground nuts.

6. Remove to cookie sheet, using metal spatula. Place in freezer until glaze is frozen, about 30 minutes.

7. If you are not serving in 30 minutes, follow instructions for wrapping for freezer on page 94.

Makes 6 to 8 balls

jell-o gelatin desserts

PLAIN AND FANCY

You can perform a lot of dessert tricks with fruit-flavored gelatin. What you cook depends upon how quickly you want to eat. Look at the approximate time for each recipe and then decide.

here's what you need

For quick-setting Jell-O

1 package Jell-O gelatin
(3 ounces), any flavor

1 cup boiling water

8 to 10 ice cubes

For jellied bananas

1 package strawberry-
banana Jell-O gelatin (3 ounces)

1 cup boiling water

12 to 14 ice cubes

1 medium ripe banana

1 table knife

For both

mixing bowl

wooden mixing spoons

here's what you do

QUICK-SETTING JELL-O

1. Boil water in tea kettle or saucepan with pouring spout.

2. Unwrap package of Jell-O directly over mixing bowl.

3. Measure 1 cup boiling water. Add to Jell-O. Stir until powder is dissolved.

4. Add ice cubes. Stir until Jell-O thickens, about 3 to 5 minutes. Remove unmelted ice.

5. Pour into serving dishes. Chill in refrigerator until firm, about 15 minutes.

Makes 4 servings

JELLIED BANANAS

Follow instructions above through Step 3.

4. Add ice cubes. Stir until Jell-O starts to thicken. Remove unmelted ice.

5. Slice bananas into serving dishes, about ½ banana per serving. Cover with thickened Jell-O.

6. Chill in refrigerator about 30 minutes. Will not be as firm as first recipe.

Makes 5 servings

funny-face cupcakes

The kids in my cooking classes and I are most grateful for the excellent cake mixes available. Choose whatever flavor you like for this recipe. Compare prices, and get the best buy.

here's what you need

package of cake mix

usually 1 or 2 eggs—check instructions on package

¼ cup butter at room temperature (½ stick)

about 1¾ cups sifted confectioners' sugar

2 to 3 tablespoons milk

1 teaspoon vanilla

raisins, almonds, any decoration

electric mixer or rotary egg beater

2 mixing bowls

2 12-cup muffin tins

paper cups for lining tins

wooden mixing spoon

measuring spoon

narrow spatula or table knife

cake rack, 1 or 2

here's what you do

1. Place two racks in oven evenly spaced. Preheat oven to temperature shown on package, usually 375°.

2. Place paper cups in muffin tins.

3. Prepare and bake cupcakes as directed on package. Pans should be staggered on two shelves so that one is not directly under another. While cupcakes are baking, make frosting.

4. Cream softened butter, which means stir butter until soft and waxy.

5. Add 1 cup confectioners' sugar gradually, stirring constantly, or use low speed on mixer.

6. Add ¾ cup confectioners' sugar, gradually alternating with milk and vanilla. Stir until smooth.

7. Cover and set aside until cupcakes are ready for frosting.

71

8. When cupcakes are baked, remove from oven, using hot pads. Place on rack for 10 minutes. Turn pan over slowly and remove cupcakes. Place them upright immediately.

9. Frost when cool, about 10 minutes after removing from pan. Place small amount of frosting on each cupcake and spread evenly.

10. Decorate immediately with raisins for eyes, almonds for a nose before frosting becomes stiff. Use other decorations if you wish.

Makes 24 cupcakes

peanut butter bar cookies

When you are baking cookies, be especially careful to follow the baking times.

here's what you need

cookies   1 cup all-purpose flour

1 cup quick-cooking oatmeal

½ cup sugar   1 egg

½ cup firmly packed brown sugar

½ teaspoon baking soda

⅓ cup peanut butter

72   ½ cup butter or margarine

about 1 tablespoon margarine for greasing pan

frosting   ½ of 16½-ounce can prepared vanilla frosting
               or
2 cups of the frosting given you on page 71

¼ cup peanut butter

fork, whisk, or hand beater

mixing bowls and spoon

baking dish 9 x 13 inches

cake rack or asbestos pad

table knife or spatula

here's what you do

1. Place oven rack in center. Preheat oven to 350°.

2. Grease pan.

3. Measure all ingredients listed (except egg) and combine in large bowl.

4. Break egg into small bowl. Beat lightly with fork, whisk, or hand beater so that white and yolk are blended. Add to mixture.

5. With fingers or mixing spoon, mix until crumbly.

6. Press cookie mixture firmly into greased pan.

7. Place in oven. Bake 20 to 25 minutes. Use hot pads to remove from oven. Place on rack to cool. You may need help from an adult at this point.
   To make certain that cookies are done, insert cake tester or toothpick in center of pan. If it comes out clean and dry, cookies are done. If not, replace in oven for a few minutes. Test again.

8. You can hurry the cooling process by placing pan in refrigerator after ten minutes on rack. In the meantime, prepare the frosting:
   Combine ½ can frosting, or 2 cups frosting as shown on page 71 with peanut butter. Beat until smooth with wooden spoon.

9. Spread frosting over cooled cookies. Cut into 2-inch squares.

Makes 24 squares

raisin pudding

You'll like this easy-to-make pudding.

here's what you need

2 slices white bread

butter, softened

¼ cup sugar

½ cup seedless raisins

1 package vanilla instant
pudding mix (4 ounces)

2 cups milk

½ teaspoon nutmeg

knife to spread the butter

spoon to sprinkle sugar

shallow 1-quart dish

1-quart mixing bowl

measuring cup

measuring spoons

strainer

egg beater

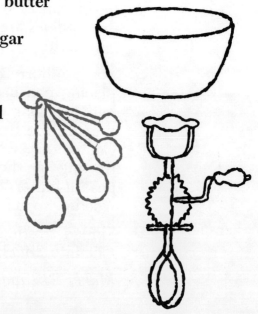

here's what you do

1. Toast bread. Butter while hot and immediately sprinkle evenly with sugar. Break into small pieces and drop into shallow dish that is large enough for the pudding.

2. Raisins for cooking are easily made plump and delicious by pouring ½ cup hot water over them. Let stand while you prepare the pudding.

3. Make the pudding according to the directions on the package.

4. Drain raisins through a strainer, shake the strainer once or twice, and then stir raisins gently into the pudding. Immediately pour the pudding over the sugared toast bites.

5. Sprinkle with nutmeg.

wacky cake

Wacky is right. The preparation is wild, but the result is delicious.

here's what you need

1⅓ cups presifted flour

1 cup sugar

3 tablespoons cocoa

1 teaspoon baking soda

½ teaspoon salt

6 tablespoons vegetable oil

1 tablespoon vinegar

1 tablespoon vanilla

1 cup cold water

whipped cream or confectioners' sugar

2-quart shallow baking pan

2-cup measuring cup

measuring spoons

fork or whisk

sifter

here's what you do

1. Place rack in center of oven and pre-heat to 375°. Lightly grease pan.

2. Tear off square of wax paper and place underneath sifter. We are using presifted flour, sometimes called "instantized," for convenience, but it is necessary to sift all of the dry ingredients together for thorough blending.

3. Measure carefully, using measuring cups and spoons, and place in sifter: —flour, sugar, cocoa, baking soda, and salt.

4. Sift these dry ingredients directly into baking pan.

5. Make three holes, spaced evenly, in dry ingredients.

6. Into the first, pour vegetable oil; into the second, vinegar; into the third, vanilla.

7. Now for the surprise, pour the cold water over all.

8. Stir with fork or whisk until blended.

9. Bake ¾ to 1 hour. Test with cake tester as described on page73.

10. Serve warm with whipped cream or confectioners' sugar on top.

things to remember

Measure exactly for desserts—there's a reason for the amounts given.

When you are baking, allow 10 to 15 minutes for the oven to reach the temperature given in recipe.

A wire whisk is a thing of joy for a cook, easy to handle and quick to clean.

In recipes calling for flour, I have given you the amount of presifted flour. Presifted flour is so convenient that I have adapted all of the recipes to its use. If you use other recipes that call for sifted flour, use the amount given less 2 tablespoons per cup.

Glass baking pans bake at 25° less than aluminum. In other words, if temperature called for is 350°, bake at 325° when using glass pans.

Confectioners' sugar should be sifted before measuring.

When recipes call for butter or margarine to be softened, this can be easily done if you remove the butter from the refrigerator in advance and allow to stand at room temperature while you get other ingredients ready.

party foods

ICE CREAM CAKE

ICE CREAM SANDWICHES

FRUIT-FLAVORED SNOWBALLS

PARTY MIX

SPICED PUNCH

ICE CREAM PUNCH

PARTY PUNCH

ice cream cake

This is a favorite for birthdays. You can buy the cake layers or make them with a cake mix.

here's what you need

1 quart ice cream of your choice (chocolate or coffee go well with the topping)

1 package whipped topping mix

1 tablespoon instant coffee powder

2 tablespoons brown sugar

2 cake layers

cake plate

wooden spoon

electric mixer, or rotary beater and bowl

measuring spoons

spatula

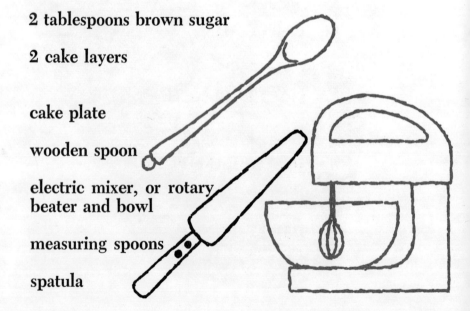

here's what you do

1. Remove lid from ice cream to let it soften for easier handling while you make the topping.

2. Prepare topping according to instructions on package, preferably with electric mixer. Remember to have an adult supervise use of electric mixer. To turn topping into amber topping, add instant coffee powder and brown sugar before whipping. Set aside until cake is ready.

3. Place cake layer on plate and spread evenly with ice cream, about 1½ inches high.

4. Top with second layer and spread ice cream.

5. Decorate top with topping.

6. Serve immediately, or cake can be placed in refrigerator for 15 to 30 minutes without ice cream melting. If you want to serve later than that, read instructions for use of freezer on page 94.

Makes 6 to 8 servings

ice cream sandwiches

Great for parties or just for you and a friend. You can make any amount you want.

here's what you need

1 pint coffee or vanilla ice cream

24 large chocolate cookies
or
24 graham crackers

tablespoon

cookie sheet or oblong
piece of heavy cardboard

here's what you do

1. Remove lid from ice cream to let it soften for easier handling.

2. Place 6 cookies or crackers in row on cookie sheet or cardboard.

3. Spoon ice cream onto each cookie and spread evenly.

4. Top with 6 cookies.

5. Before you make another 6, place those already made in refrigerator or freezer.

6. When you have finished second batch (which gives you 12) you can keep them in the refrigerator for a brief time—about 15 minutes—without melting.

7. If you want to wait longer before eating, follow instructions for storing in freezer given page 94.

Makes 12 sandwiches

fruit-flavored snowballs

Do you have a way of crushing ice? If so, this recipe is a cinch. If not, you can pound ice in a clean heavy old cloth (such as worn-out towel) with a hammer. That's fun, too. Stop a minute, though, and ask an adult where and how to do the pounding.

here's what you need

1 quart shaved or crushed ice

1 envelope soft drink mix, any flavor*

1 cup sugar

1 quart cold water

glass pitcher

1-cup measuring cup

wooden spoon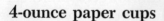

4-ounce paper cups

* There are several soft drink mixes in the store.
One of the better known is Kool-Aid.

here's what you do

1. After ice is prepared, fill 12 paper cups a little above brim. Place in refrigerator.

2. Empty package of soft drink mix into pitcher. Add sugar. Measure cold water and ice to make 2 quarts. Add to soft drink mix and stir thoroughly to dissolve.

3. Pour over ice-filled cups.

4. May be placed in freezer until party time.

Makes 12 snowballs

party mix

This is so good, the adults will borrow your recipe. On our block, the children have money-raising activities for important groups like UNICEF. Once they sold food, including this mix, and did very well. If you try it, you should each share cost of groceries.

here's what you need

½ cup margarine

1 envelope bleu cheese or garlic salad dressing mix

1 tablespoon Worcestershire sauce

2 cups bite-sized shredded wheat biscuits

2 cups bite-sized rice biscuits

2 cups ready-to-eat oat cereal

2 cups salted peanuts and 1 cup pretzel sticks

small saucepan

small custard cup

shallow baking pan called a "jelly-roll tin" although practically no one makes jelly roll any more

regular table fork

2-cup measuring cup

measuring spoons

here's what you do

1. Preheat oven to 300°.

2. Place margarine in saucepan and melt over low to medium heat. Stir occasionally while butter is melting.

3. Hold package of salad dressing mix by corner and shake several times. Mix will not spill when you open at tearing line. Pour into melted butter and stir.

4. Measure Worcestershire sauce into small custard cup and add to mix. Stir.

5. Measure and pour into shallow pan: wheat biscuits, rice biscuits, oat cereal and combined peanuts and pretzel sticks.

6. Mix thoroughly with fork until all ingredients are evenly coated. Takes several minutes.

7. Place pan in oven. Toast for total of 30 minutes.

8. Every 10 minutes, remove pan (use pot holder) and stir with fork. Return to oven until completed.

Makes 2½ quarts

spiced punch

If you are having a party in the winter, you can serve hot spiced punch. This recipe comes from Williamsburg, Virginia, an interesting restored colonial village, whose restaurants serve food prepared from early American recipes.

here's what you need

¼ cup lemon juice

1 quart apple cider or apple juice

1 teaspoon cloves

1 teaspoon nutmeg

2 cinnamon sticks

1½ quart saucepan

wooden spoon

measuring spoons

measuring cup

square of cheese cloth or clean white cloth and white string

here's what you do

1. Measure ¼ cup lemon juice and combine with apple cider or juice in sauce pan.

2. Cut square of cheese cloth, or clean white cloth, about 5 x 5 inches. Measure and place the following on cloth: cloves, nutmeg, and cinnamon sticks broken into smaller pieces. Make a bag by tying ends together with string.

3. Place saucepan over low heat, bring up to boiling point, add bag of spices, and simmer 5 to 10 minutes. Remove bag of spices.

4. Serve punch hot in gaily colored cups. (Can be served chilled.)

Makes 8 servings, about 4 ounces each

ice cream punch

This punch is a combination of ice cream and something to drink. All you need to add for a party is a plain butter cookie—nothing fancy, because the punch is very rich.

here's what you need

¼ cup instant coffee powder, or instant coffee without caffeine*

⅓ cup sugar

1 cup milk

1 bottle chilled club soda (1 pint, 12 ounces)

½ pint vanilla or coffee ice cream, softened

pretty bowl large enough to hold 2 quarts

measuring cup

mixing spoon

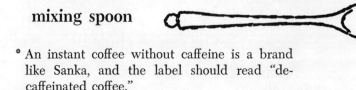

* An instant coffee without caffeine is a brand like Sanka, and the label should read "decaffeinated coffee."

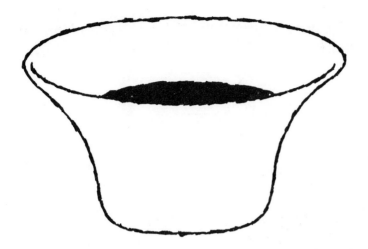

here's what you do

1. Measure coffee and sugar. Pour into bowl.

2. Measure milk and add to coffee, stirring until coffee has dissolved.

3. Add club soda.

4. Stir in ice cream.

5. Serve immediately.
   If you do not want to serve immediately, complete Step 1 and 2; then finish recipe with 3 and 4 just before guests arrive.

Makes 10 servings, about 4 ounces each

party punch

Punch is easier to serve at a party than bottled soft drinks. The punch bowl is also very gay and pretty as a centerpiece.

here's what you need

3 cups boiling water

15 tea bags

⅔ cup sugar

1 quart cold water

2 cups orange juice

1 cup bottled lemon juice

ice cubes

1½ quarts ginger ale
(1 quart, 1 pint)

large saucepan or Pyrex mixing bowl

tongs

punch bowl

here's what you do

1. Fill tea kettle with a little more than 3 cups water. Place on high heat to boil.

2. Place tea bags in largest saucepan you can find, or Pyrex mixing bowl. Add boiling water (you may need an adult to help), cover and let stand for 4 minutes.

3. Remove tea bags. Use tongs if necessary.

4. Add ⅔ cup sugar and stir until dissolved. Add cold water.

5. While tea is cooling, measure orange juice and lemon juice, and add to tea.

6. Place tea mixture in punch bowl.

7. Just before guests arrive, add 1 or 2 trays of ice cubes. Stir gently.

8. Add ginger ale.

   Makes 25 servings, about 5 ounces each

things to remember

Party food such as the ice cream cake, which has a whipped topping, should be frozen before wrapping.

Freezing food is a convenience when you are planning a party. Although you will probably not plan too far ahead, it is helpful to know that ice cream and cake may be kept 1 to 2 months and sandwiches for 2 weeks. However, you would never be able to let it stay in the freezer that long, I'm sure.

For freezing, you should have:
    sheet wrapping which is air- and moistureproof or plastic bags,
    freezer tape,
    freezer marking pencil or crayon.

The "drugstore wrap" is the easiest wrap: place food in center of wrapping. Bring front and back edges of wrap together, pulling tightly. Turn under, making about 1-inch fold, and continue folding downward until wrap hugs food. Fold edges of each end under, pressing closely to squeeze out air. Seal with freezer tape and mark date. Freeze at once.

For a punch bowl, you might want to use one of the lovely pastel-colored large Pyrex mixing bowls, or use the clear ones and wrap the outside in aluminum foil.

snacks

APRICOT COCONUT BALLS

CHUNKIES

ORANGE-SUGARED PECANS

HOMEMADE POPCORN

OVEN-SALTED NUTS

STUFFED CELERY

RAW VEGETABLE TRAY

apricot coconut balls

These are fun to prepare for yourself or as gifts for favorite friends.

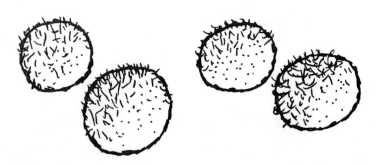

here's what you need

1½ cups dried uncooked apricots (6 ounces)

2 cups shredded coconut (2 cans, 4 ounces each)

⅔ cup sweetened condensed milk

confectioners' sugar

mixing bowl

1- or 2-cup measuring cup

mixing spoon

paper plates or wax paper

here's what you do

1. Measure and grind apricots in blender. (Grinding takes only 1 or 2 minutes because the blades of the blender are powerful. Let an adult be ready to help with blender.) If you do not have a blender, chop apricots on chopping board with paring knife or cut with scissors.

2. Place ground apricots in mixing bowl.

3. Measure coconut and add to apricots.

4. Measure condensed milk and pour into mixing bowl.

5. Stir until blended.

6. Pour 1 cup presifted confectioners' sugar on paper plate or wax paper. Place second paper plate or wax paper in line for finished apricot coconut balls.

7. Shape apricot mixture into small balls, about the size of a walnut, roll in sugar, place on paper plate. Let stand until firm, about 1 hour.

Number of servings depends on size of balls

chunkies

A candy thermometer is handy for this recipe, but you can manage without it.

here's what you need

1 cup dark corn syrup

Butter for greasing

5 cups prepared mixed cereal such as alphabet oat cereal, corn flakes, or any combination of unsweetened cereal

½ cup unsalted Spanish peanuts

1 teaspoon vinegar

1-quart saucepan

large bowl

candy thermometer

wooden spoon

measuring spoons

2 1-cup measuring cups

shallow pan

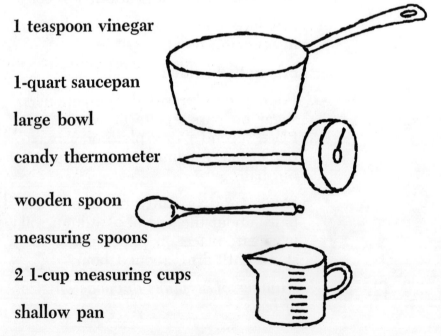

here's what you do

1. Measure corn syrup and pour into saucepan.

2. Place on medium heat. Boil until syrup reaches 242° on candy thermometer, or until it forms a firm ball in cold water. To do this: drop teaspoon of syrup into cold water, which will cool and thicken syrup. Shape into ball. Firm ball is easily shaped between fingers and keeps shape when removed from water. Make this test about 5 minutes after syrup begins to boil.

3. While syrup is boiling, butter bowl and shallow pan.

4. Measure and pour cereal and nuts into bowl.

5. After syrup has reached proper temperature, remove from heat, measure, and stir in vinegar.

6. Pour syrup over cereal and stir vigorously.

7. Pack into greased pan and let chunkies harden.

8. Break into small pieces, about 2 inches in size.

Makes 10 to 12 servings

orange-sugared pecans

Candied pecans are a different-tasting treat. They're easy to make. You can use walnuts, if you prefer.

here's what you need

1 orange

½ cup orange juice

1½ cups sugar

2½ cups pecan halves

1½-quart saucepan

mixing spoon

1-cup measuring cup

2-cup measuring cup

measuring spoons

wax paper

grater

asbestos pad or wooden chopping board

here's what you do

1. Wash and dry orange. Hold firmly in one hand with grater held in other on piece of wax paper. Rub orange against grater, shifting the orange as you remove the peel. Measure 1 tablespoon peel and set aside.

2. Squeeze juice from orange and measure ½ cup.

3. Measure sugar and combine with orange juice in saucepan, and place over medium heat.

4. Cook to 240°, or soft-ball stage. A soft-ball stage means that the syrup (for that's what you are making) collects into one mass, is made into a soft ball between finger tips, and stays together when lifted out of water.

5. When this stage is reached, remove saucepan from heat and place on asbestos pad or wooden chopping board.

6. Measure pecan halves. Add to syrup along with grated orange peel. Stir until syrup looks cloudy.

7. Drop by teaspoons on wax paper. Allow to cool.

Makes 36 to 48 pieces

homemade popcorn

Thank the American Indians for this treat. How you pop corn depends upon where you are and what utensils you have.

here's what you need

vegetable oil or shortening

1 can unpopped corn
(10 ounces)

butter if you wish

salt

electric skillet or popper
   or
for cooking on gas or
electric range, you will
need deep heavy frying
pan with airtight cover
   or
for cooking over wood or
coal embers, you will need
long-handled wire popper

here's what you do

If you are using gas or electric range:

1. Place heavy frying pan on medium heat.

2. Pour in enough oil to cover bottom of pan, about 2 tablespoons. Heat for 3 to 4 minutes.

3. Lower heat and add ⅓ to ½ cup un-popped corn.

4. Cover and shake gently. Do not peek at this stage.

5. Melt butter in small saucepan over low heat while popcorn is popping.

6. Uncover frying pan when all sounds of popping have stopped, about 10 minutes.

7. Pour popcorn into bowl, sprinkle with salt, and pour in melted butter. Stir or shake gently.

If you are using an electric popper, the instructions come with it.

If you want to pop corn over coals or wood embers of a campfire, you need a long-handled wire popper. Pour corn into wire basket, fasten se-curely, and shake gently over coals.

1 cup unpopped corn makes 5 cups

oven-salted nuts

Of course the grocer's shelves are filled with snacks, but it's fun to make your own. Use any nuts you like, and for mixed nuts bake each variety separately and then mix.

here's what you need

3 cups shelled nuts

1 tablespoon butter

salt plus a small amount of chili powder or a choice of herbs and spices mentioned on next page. Read carefully.

shallow pan

asbestos pad or wooden chopping board

here's what you do

1. Preheat oven to 350°.

2. Measure nuts.

3. Measure butter.

4. Remove pan from oven and place on asbestos pad or wooden chopping board. Arrange nuts in one layer in pan.

5. Sprinkle with salt, plus a little chili powder.

6. If you feel adventuresome, try celery or herb seasoning which usually is combined with salt. Or you can add curry powder, cumin, or oregano along with the salt.
   The following are combinations of herbs and salt, so if you want to try them, skip the salt:
   > hickory smoke salt or herb seasoning salt or onion salt

7. Bake 20 minutes, turning with spatula every 10 minutes. Can be served hot or cold.

Makes 3 cups

stuffed celery

I get the feeling from the talk in my older classes that kids are beginning to understand about nutrition, that good eating habits can make a difference in strength and co-ordination. One of the great eating habits is munching raw vegetables. Try combining two health-giving foods like cheese and celery in this recipe for stuffed celery.

here's what you need

celery stalks

cream cheese and chives
           or
any of the process-cheese spreads

cutting board

paring knife

spreader

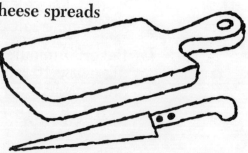

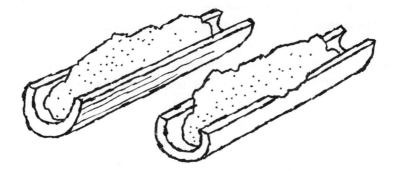

here's what you do

1. To trim celery: cut off thin piece at bottom of whole stalk. Separate stalks, scrub with vegetable brush under cold running water, and drain. If outer stalks are tough, place in plastic bag to be used for cooking. Often, however, they are as tender as inner stalks.

2. To freshen, if celery is wilted, place in deep bowl of ice water.

3. After celery is drained and dried, fill stalks with cheese of your choice.

4. Can be served or eaten immediately, or you may keep celery fresh in refrigerator for many hours by covering with airtight transparent wrap.

Allow 1 or 2 stalks per person

raw vegetable tray

Raw vegetables have a completely different flavor than cooked vegetables—so different that you will find it hard to believe. Fix a tray of several vegetables to nibble on while you're reading. Line tray with napkin or paper mat. Place a basket of salted Spanish peanuts on one side of tray and line up salted vegetables on the other.

here's what you need

carrots

cauliflower

cucumbers

tray or platter

vegetable parer

paring knife

large mixing bowl

ice

chopping board

fork

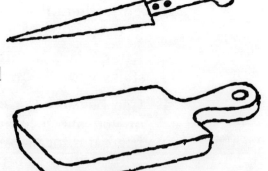

here's what you do

Fill large bowl with ice.

For carrot curls

1. Scrub with brush under cool running water.
2. Remove slice at top of carrot.
3. With vegetable parer, make long straight strips from top to bottom.
4. Curl each strip around finger; carefully remove curl and place on ice. Let stand while preparing other vegetables.

For cauliflowerets

1. Remove outside leaves from head of cauliflower.
2. Wash under cool running water.
3. Break head into small flowerets.
4. Place on ice to chill, but do not move carrot curls.

For cucumber slices

1. Peel cucumber.
2. If you want a pretty effect, run fork down length of cucumber from end to end.
3. Place on chopping board and cut crosswise into thin slices.

things to remember

1 teaspoon$=\frac{1}{3}$ tablespoon

1 tablespoon$=3$ teaspoons

$\frac{1}{3}$ cup$=5\frac{1}{3}$ tablespoons

$\frac{1}{4}$ cup$=4$ tablespoons

1 cup liquid$=8$ ounces$=$ 16 tablespoons

1 ounce liquid$=2$ tablespoons

$\frac{7}{8}$ cup$=1$ cup minus 2 tablespoons

$\frac{1}{4}$ pound stick butter$=$ $\frac{1}{2}$ cup

1 pound box confectioners' sugar$=3\frac{1}{2}$ cups

regional cooking

CALIFORNIA—
AVOCADO SALAD

COLORADO—
DENVER SANDWICHES

MIDWESTERN STATES—
APPLE BROWN BETTY

NEW ENGLAND—
BAKED BEANS

PENNSYLVANIA—
DUTCH FUNNEL CAKE

SOUTHERN STATES—
HOMINY GRITS

TEXAS—
BARBECUE SAUCE

california avocado salad (guacamole)

Regional cooking grew in our country because of the food habits of the original settlers and the availability of certain foods. Foods are almost always a little cheaper where they are grown, so lucky Californians can enjoy avocados more than those of us in the East. Guacamole (gwa-ca-mol) can be served as a first course, in a salad on lettuce leaves, or as a dip surrounded by corn chips.

here's what you need

1 large ripe avocado

2 teaspoons lemon juice*

½ teaspoon garlic salt, or more

½ teaspoon chili powder, or more

2 or more tablespoons mayonnaise

table knife

kitchen fork

measuring spoons

wooden mixing spoon

mixing bowl

* Use bottled lemon juice

here's what you do

1. To peel avocado, cut in half lengthwise, using ordinary table knife. If avocado is soft, halves will come apart immediately; if not, turn halves slightly to get them apart. Remove seed. Cut off shell with paring knife, or use back of teaspoon to pry off shell.

2. Sprinkle avocado immediately with lemon juice to keep from turning dark.

3. Place avocado in shallow mixing bowl and mash thoroughly.

4. Measure and add garlic salt, chili powder, and mayonnaise. Mix thoroughly with fork. Taste and see if you want to add more seasoning. It's a personal choice.

5. Serve on lettuce leaves for salad or appetizer; serve in bowl surrounded by corn chips for dip.

Makes about 3 to 4 servings as salad or appetizer

colorado

denver sandwiches

They really do eat Denver sandwiches in Denver and, as a matter of fact, all over the West.

here's what you need

½ pound sliced bacon

2 medium-sized onions

1 green pepper

½ cup chopped ham
(this is optional)

8 eggs

salt and pepper

butter, softened

8 slices of bread

chopping board

paring knife

large kitchen spoon

pancake turner

frying pan

egg beater

here's what you do

1. Place bacon on chopping board and cut slices into ½-inch pieces. Place in frying pan and cook until light brown over medium heat.

2. While bacon is frying, chop onions as mentioned on page 49.

3. Chop green pepper.

4. Cook onions and green pepper briefly, about 2 minutes, or until onions begin to look limp.

5. Remove frying pan from heat and with large kitchen spoon remove excess bacon grease, leaving about 1 tablespoon to keep eggs from sticking. Return frying pan to low heat.

6. Beat eggs with rotary beater. Pour into frying pan over onions, bacon, and green pepper. Stir gently. Add ham, if desired.

7. When lightly browned, turn; cut into 4 wedges; and serve between slices of buttered bread.

Makes 4 sandwiches

midwestern states
apple brown betty

In the early days of our country, John Chapman (nick-named Johnny Appleseed) traveled through the Ohio wilderness preaching sermons and planting apple seeds. Because of Johnny Appleseed, according to the legend, we have many apple orchards in the Midwestern states. Apples are, of course, grown in many other areas, but you will find that cooked apple recipes, such as apple brown Betty, seem to appear more frequently in the Midwest.

here's what you need

6 slices white bread

½ cup butter (1 stick)   1 teaspoon cinnamon

¾ cup brown sugar   ⅛ teaspoon salt

2 pounds tart green apples

¼ cup bottled lemon juice

fat for greasing casserole

2-quart casserole

saucepan

measuring spoons

1-cup measuring cup

4-cup measuring cup

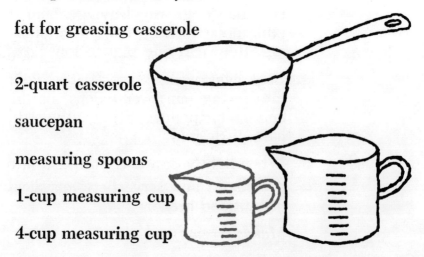

here's what you do

1. Preheat oven to 350°.

2. Grease casserole.

3. Tear bread slices in small pieces.

4. Melt butter in saucepan over low heat.

5. Remove from heat. Add bread crumbs and stir.

6. Measure dry ingredients and stir into crumbs the brown sugar, cinnamon, and salt.

7. Peel and slice enough tart green apples to measure 5 cups. Sprinkle with lemon juice after each cup to keep apples from discoloring.

8. Layer apples and crumb mixture in casserole, ending with crumbs.

9. Pour ⅓ cup water over apple mixture. Cover and bake ½ hour. Uncover and continue to bake ½ hour.

Makes 6 servings

new england
baked beans

The long cooking of New England baked beans began because church-going Yankees started the Sabbath on Saturday night, which meant doing all work, including cooking, before that time, so that Sunday was indeed a day of rest. Beans were soaked Friday night, cooked all day Saturday, and served for Saturday night supper, Sunday breakfast, and all day Sunday. I'm going to give you a shortened version of the recipe, but baked beans do need a certain amount of time for baking.

here's what you need

1 can pork and beans (1 pound, 12 ounces)

¼ cup catchup

2 tablespoons brown sugar

2 tablespoons molasses

1 tablespoon onion powder

1½ teaspoons prepared mustard

1½-quart casserole

measuring spoons

mixing spoon

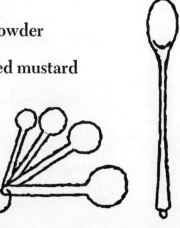

here's what you do

1. Preheat oven to 300°.
2. Grease casserole lightly.
3. Open and pour can pork and beans into casserole.
4. Measure and stir into beans: catchup, brown sugar, molasses, onion powder, and prepared mustard.
5. Bake covered for 1 hour; lower heat and bake uncovered for additional hour.

Makes 4 servings

pennsylvania
dutch funnel cakes

The Pennsylvania Dutch country centers around the town of Lancaster in the eastern part of the state. The people there are of German origin, not Dutch. They work hard on their rich farming land and enjoy the food that comes from it. The recipe for Dutch funnel cakes is especially fun to prepare because of the use of the funnel.

here's what you need

1⅓ cups presifted flour   2 tablespoons sugar

1 teaspoon baking powder   ⅛ teaspoon salt

1 quart vegetable oil for frying

⅔ cup milk   1 egg

confectioners' sugar or molasses

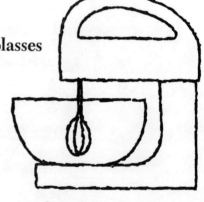

electric frying pan or
standard frying pan

mixing bowl and rotary
beater or electric mixer

fork

2-cup measuring cup

measuring spoons

medium-sized funnel

here's what you do

1. Measure flour into a 2-cup measuring cup. Measure the sugar, salt, and baking powder into flour. Stir with fork to blend dry ingredients.

2. Add enough vegetable oil to frying pan to measure at least 2 inches. Heat to 375°.

3. Break egg into medium-sized mixing bowl. Measure and add ⅔ cup milk.

4. Beat lightly with electric mixer or rotary beater.

5. Add dry ingredients and beat until smooth.

6. Hold finger over spout of funnel, or place a piece of foil to close it. Spoon batter into funnel.

7. Drop batter into frying pan by removing finger from bottom of funnel. Let batter slide through, swirling into circles from center out. Each cake should be about 3 inches in diameter. Work close to frying pan and fat will not splatter.

8. Fry until golden brown. Drain on paper towel and serve immediately with confectioners' sugar or molasses.

Makes 9 to 10 cakes, depending on size

southern states
hominy grits

Grits are one of our oldest foods. People have been eating grits since they first grew corn and learned to grind the corn themselves or brought it to the village mill to be ground. Today it is eaten mostly in our Southern states. Grits are excellent for breakfast with scrambled eggs, or good at any meal as a substitute for potatoes. Always top with butter.

122

here's what you need

1 cup hominy grits*

salt

butter

1½-quart saucepan

* Grits are usually found on the grocery shelves in the cereal section.

here's what you do

1. Measure and pour 4 cups water into saucepan.

2. Bring to boil over high heat.

3. Pour grits slowly into boiling water. Stir until mixture boils. Lower heat immediately. Add salt, cover, and simmer 1 hour, stirring frequently.

4. When ready to serve, top with a pat of butter.

Makes 4 to 6 servings

texas
barbecue sauce

Down in Texas eating habits are influenced by the spicy food served by their Mexican neighbors. Texas barbecue sauce is a fine example of their liking for south-of-the-border food. You may brush hamburgers with sauce during cooking or pour heated sauce over hamburgers when done. It goes well over other meats, chicken, or eggs.

here's what you need

2 cups catchup

⅔ cups Worcestershire sauce

½ cup vinegar

1 teaspoon salt

⅛ teaspoon cayenne pepper

2 tablespoons vegetable oil

2 garlic cloves

frying pan or saucepan, at least 6-cup size

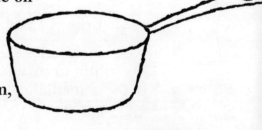

2-cup measuring cup

measuring spoons

here's what you do

1. Measure and pour into saucepan the catchup, Worcestershire sauce, vinegar, salt, cayenne pepper, and vegetable oil.

2. Peel garlic cloves and add to mixture.

3. Bring liquid to boil over medium heat. Lower heat and simmer for 20 minutes. Remove and throw away garlic cloves.

Makes 3½ cups

index

127